Easy Classics For Piano Solo

CLASSICAL GREATS

You've Always Wanted To Play

Published by
Chester Music
14-15 Berners Street, London W1T 3LJ, UK.

Exclusive Distributors:
Music Sales Limited
Distribution Centre, Newmarket Road, Bury St Edmunds,
Suffolk IP33 3YB, UK.
Music Sales Corporation
257 Park Avenue South, New York, NY 10010, USA.
Music Sales Pty Limited
20 Resolution Drive, Caringbah, NSW 2229, Australia.

Order No. CH74261
ISBN: 978-1-84772-745-9
This book © Copyright 2008 Chester Music.

Compiled and edited by Jenni Wheeler
Arranged and engraved by Camden Music
Printed in the EU

This publication is not authorised for sale in France and Mexico.

CHESTER MUSIC
part of The Music Sales Group
London / New York / Paris / Sydney / Copenhagen / Berlin / Madrid / Tokyo

Adagio Cantabile
(from 'Sonata Pathétique', Op.13)

Music by Ludwig Van Beethoven

Adagio for Strings

Music by Samuel Barber

Air
(from 'Water Music')

Music by George Frideric Handel

11

Allegro
(from 'Sonata Facile' in C Major, K545)

Music by Wolfgang Amadeus Mozart

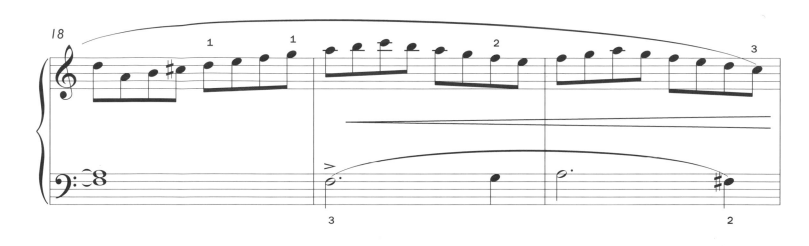

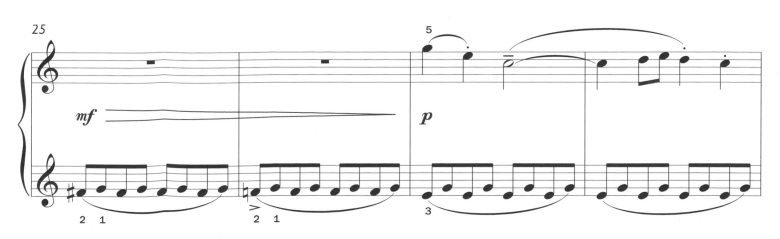

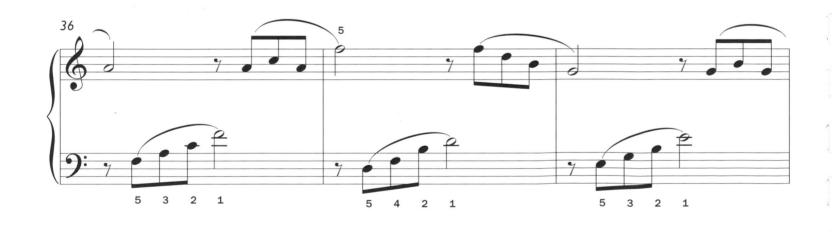

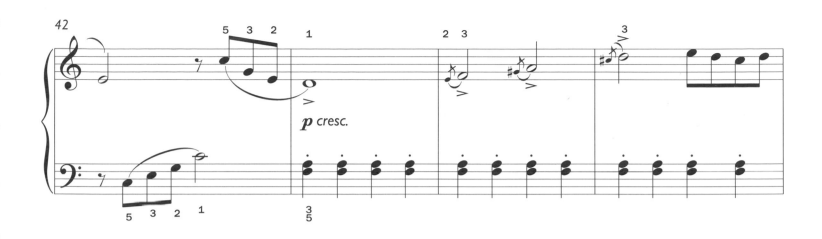

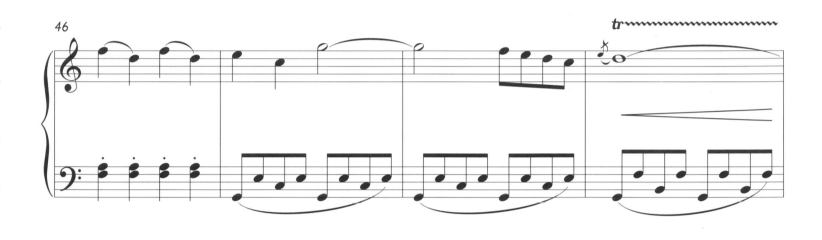

Andante
(from 'Symphony No.3')

Music by Johannes Brahms

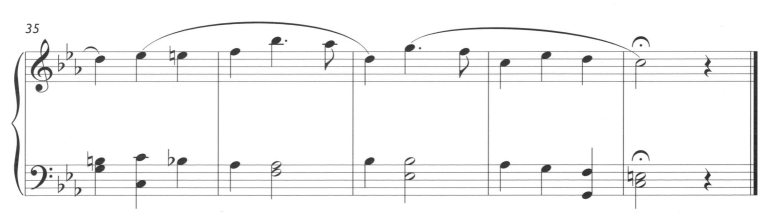

The Arrival Of The Queen Of Sheba

Music by George Frideric Handel

Autumn
(from 'The Four Seasons', 3rd movement)

Music by Antonio Vivaldi

Barcarolle
(from 'The Tales Of Hoffmann')

Music by Jacques Offenbach

Moderato

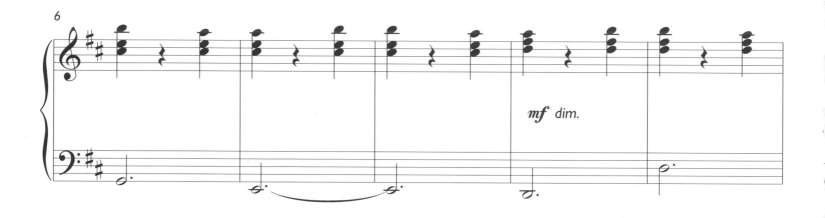

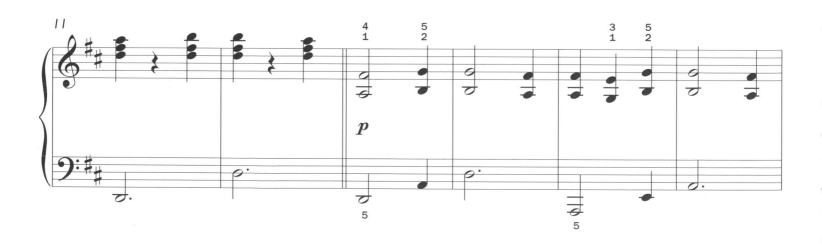

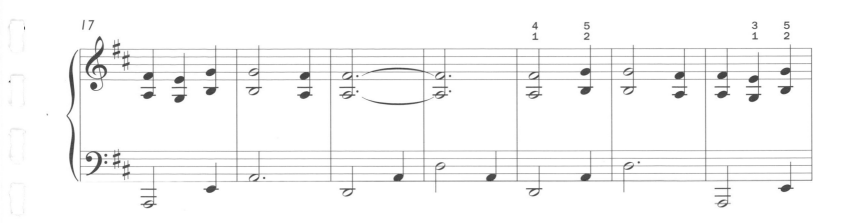

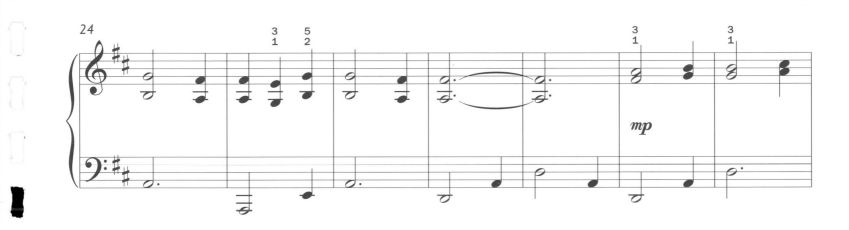

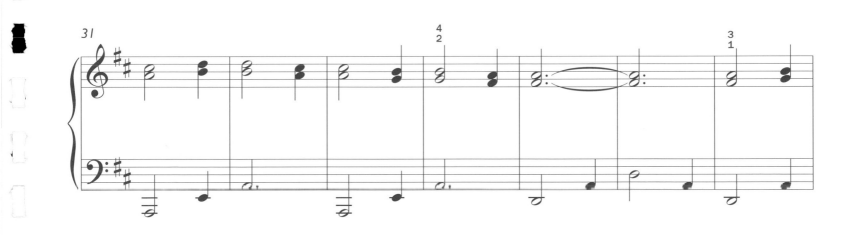

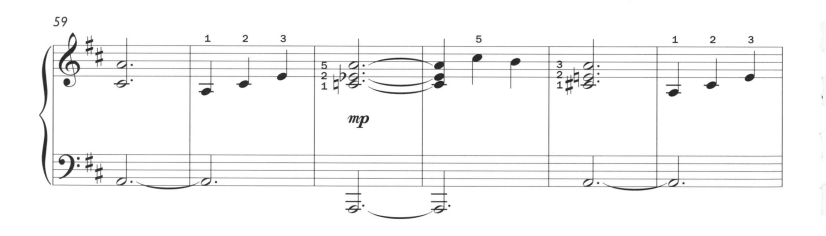

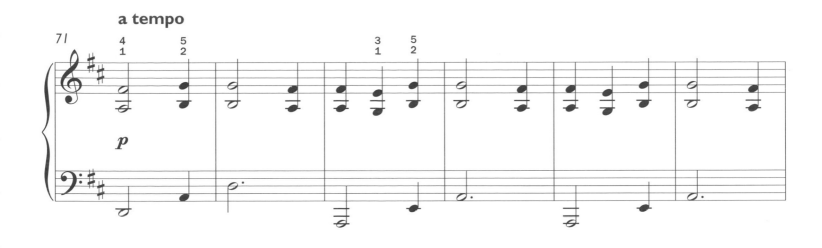

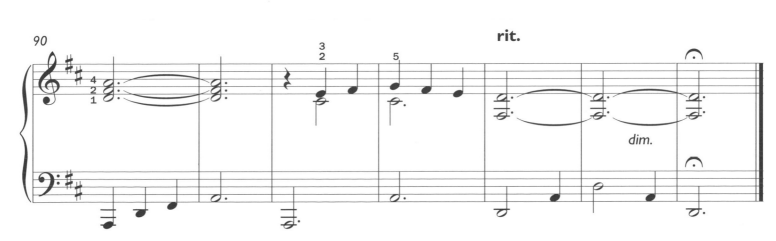

The Blue Danube

Music by Johann Strauss II

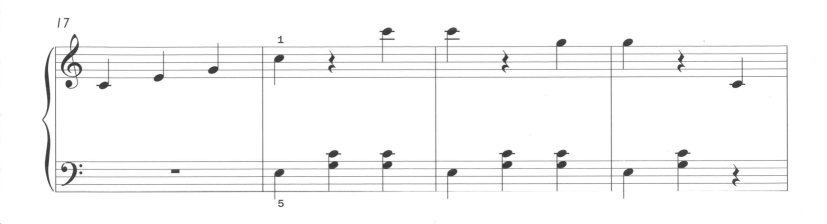

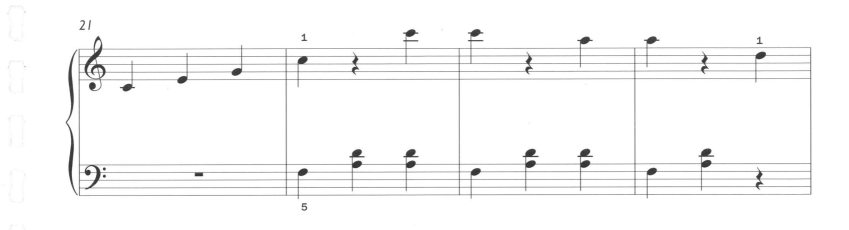

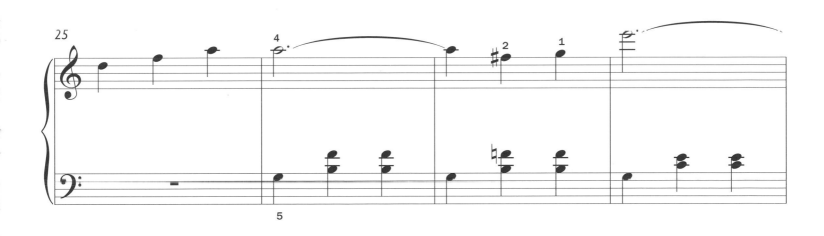

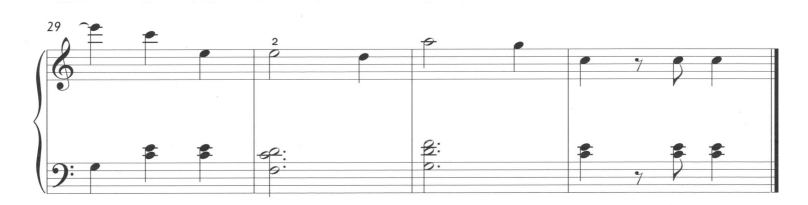

Canon in D

Music by Johann Pachelbel

Dance Of The Sylphs
(from 'The Damnation Of Faust')

Music by Hector Berlioz

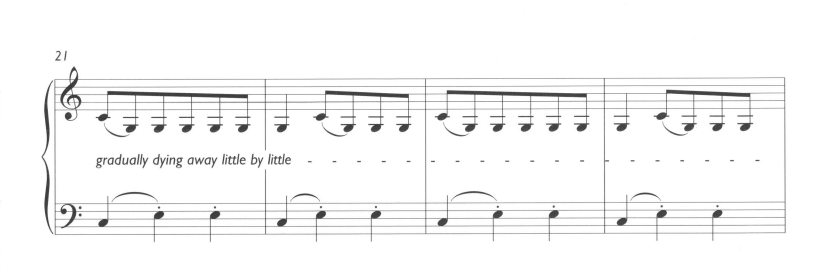

gradually dying away little by little –

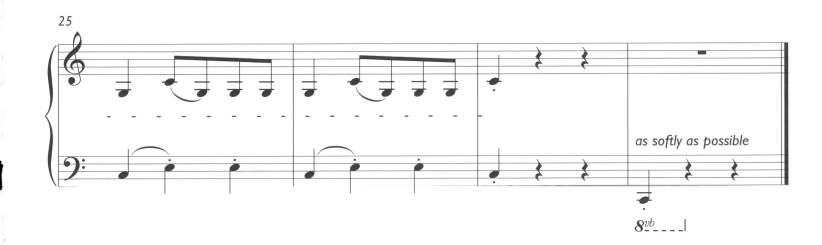

as softly as possible

8vb _ _ _ _ |

Die Moldau
(from 'Ma Vlast')

Music by Bedrich Smetana

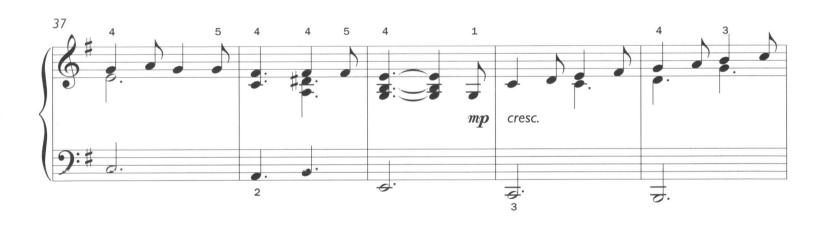

Eine Kleine Nachtmusik, K525
(1st movement: Allegro)

Music by Wolfgang Amadeus Mozart

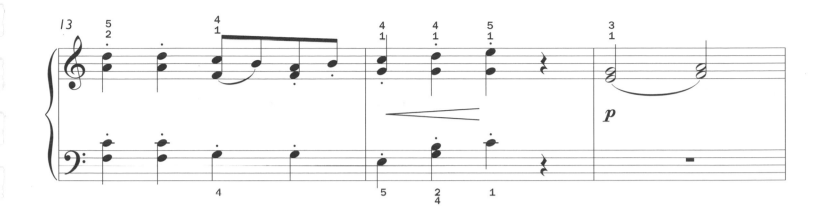

Fantaisie Impromptu

Music by Frédéric Chopin

Con espressione e legato

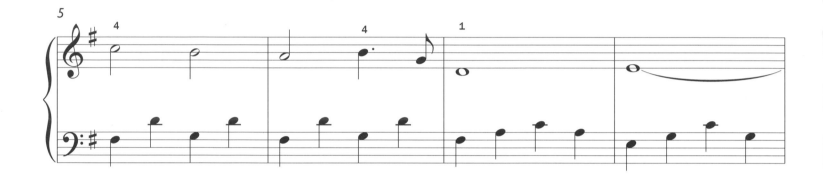

Flower Duet
(from 'Lakmé')

Music by Léo Delibes

Für Elise

Music by Ludwig Van Beethoven

Moderato

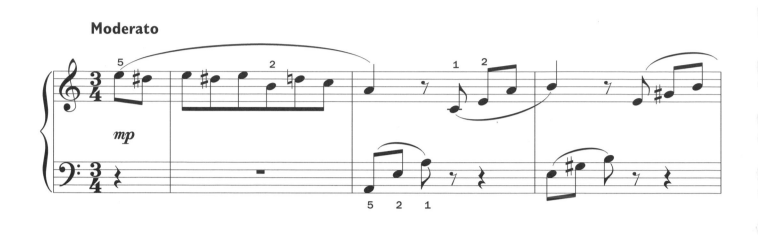

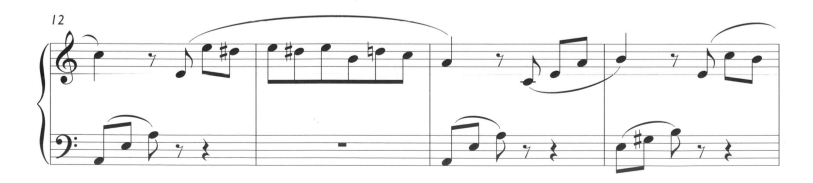

The Hebrides Overture
('Fingal's Cave')

Music by Felix Mendelssohn Bartholdy

Humoresque

Music by Antonín Dvořák

Allegretto

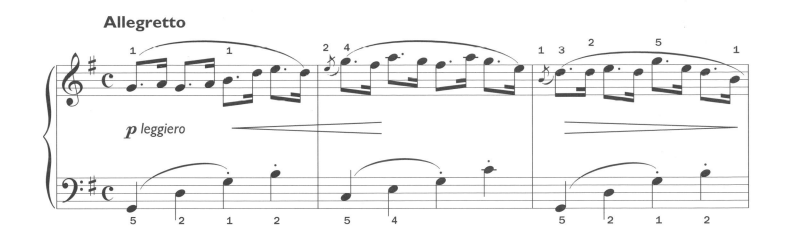

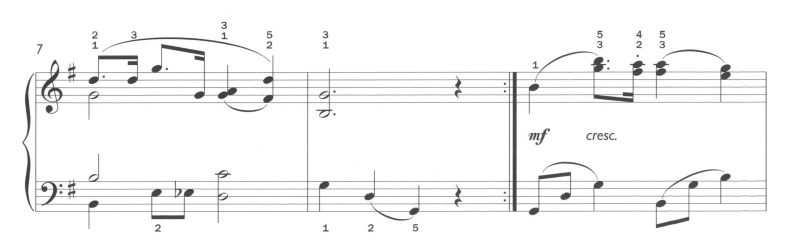

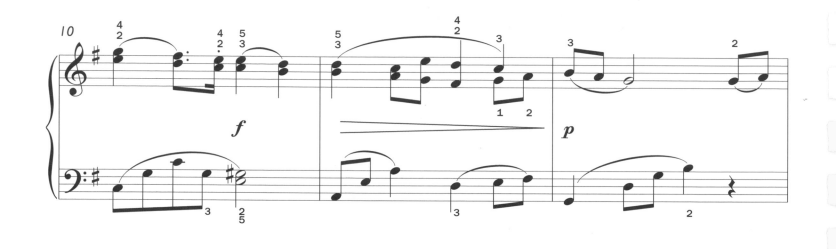

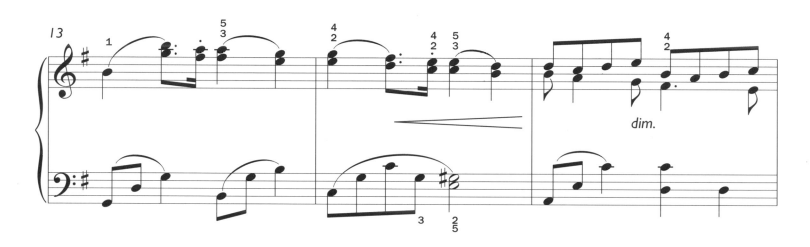

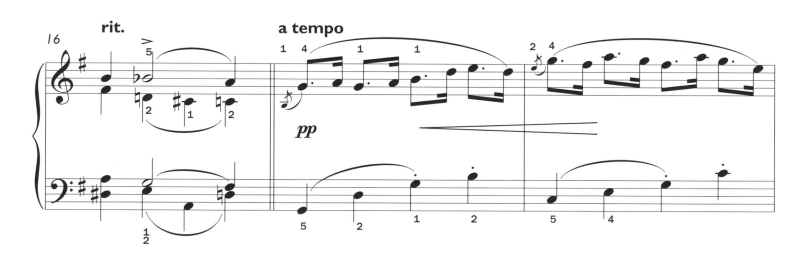

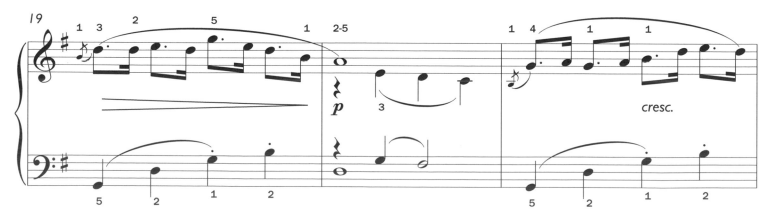

54

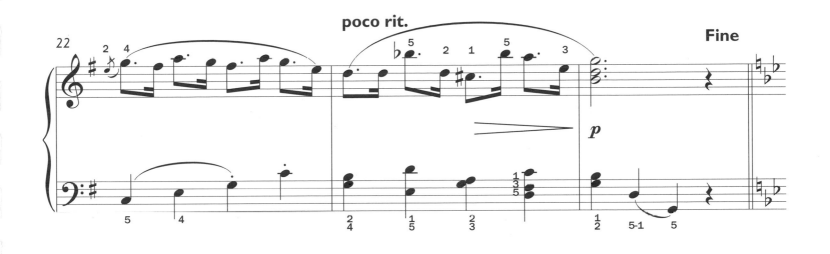

Jesu, Joy Of Man's Desiring

Music by Johann Sebastian Bach

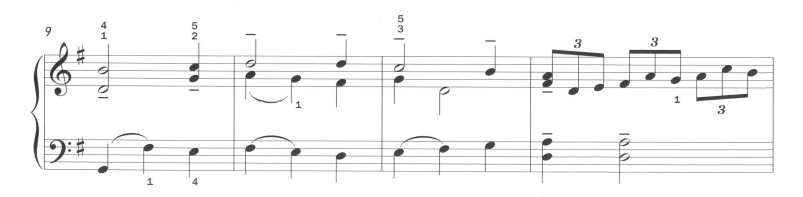

rall. poco a poco

Largo
(from 'Xerxes')

Music by George Frideric Handel

La Donna É Mobile

Music by Giuseppe Verdi

Larghetto

Music by Domenico Scarlatti

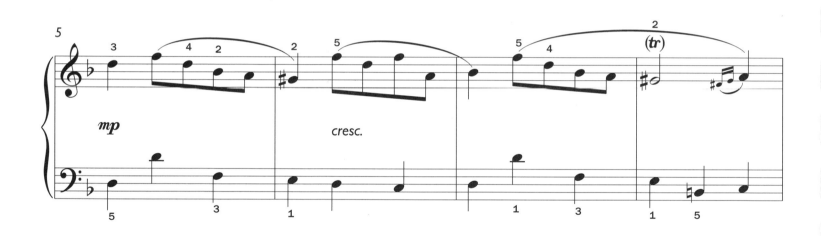

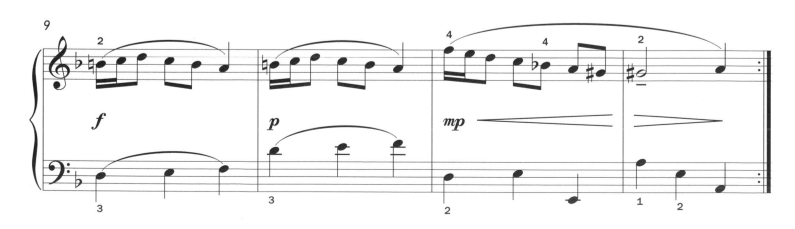

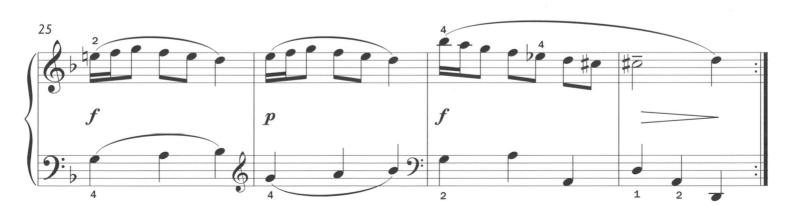

Little Fugue

Music by Domenico Zipoli

rit.

Lullaby

Music by Johannes Brahms

dim. e rall. al fine

Mazurka Op.67, No.2

Music by Frédéric Chopin

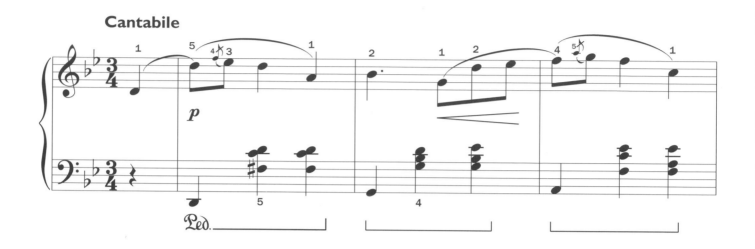

Ped. come sopra

Minuet
(from 'String Quartet')

Music by Luigi Boccherini

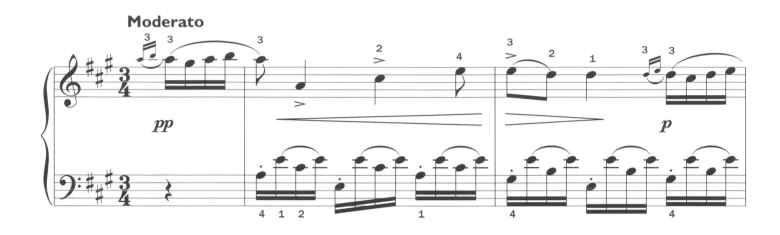

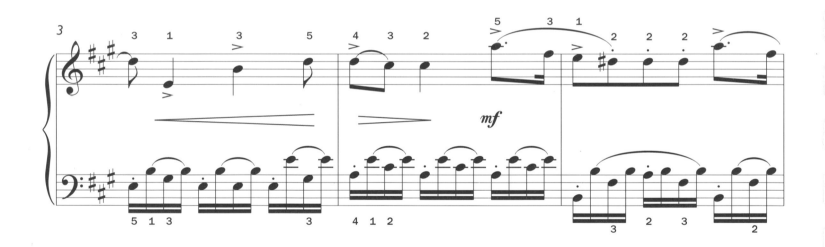

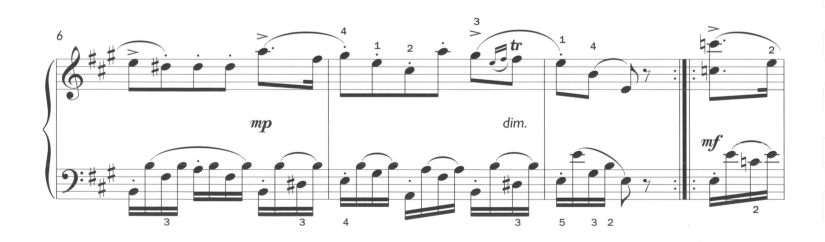

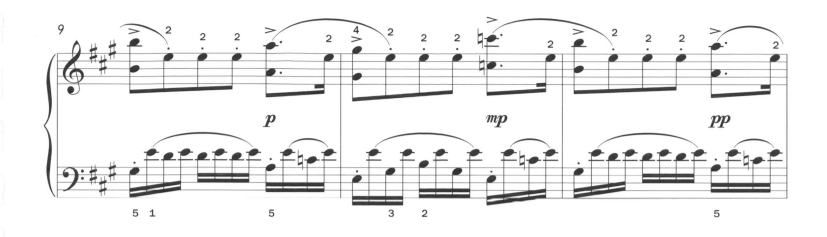

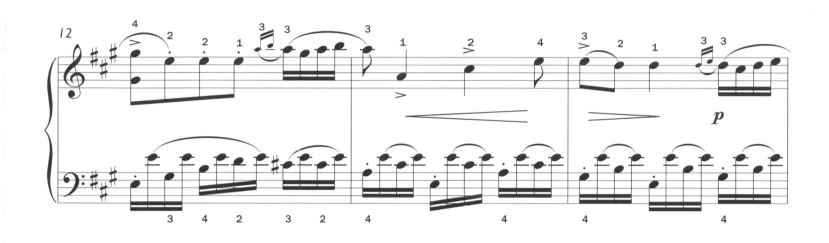

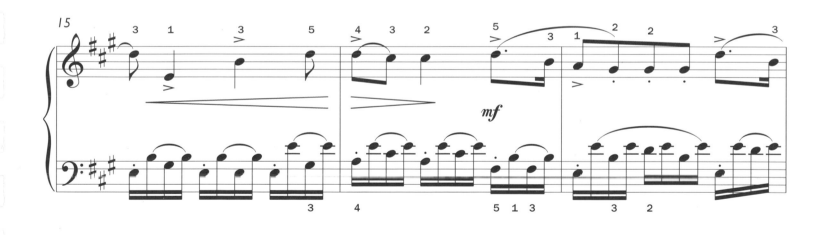

Fine

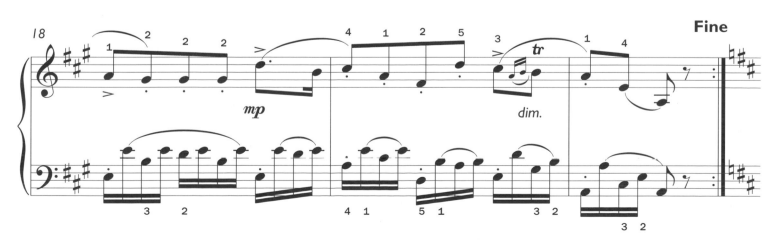

D.C. al Fine
(after repeat)

Minuet in G Major

Music by Ludwig Van Beethoven

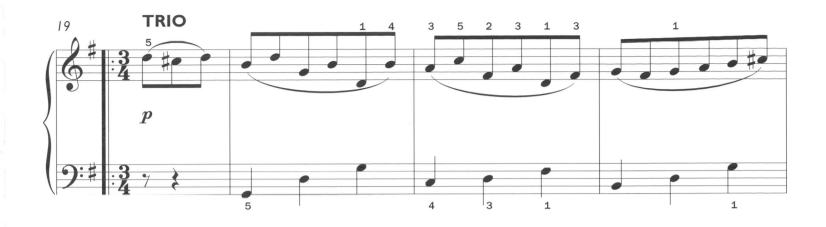

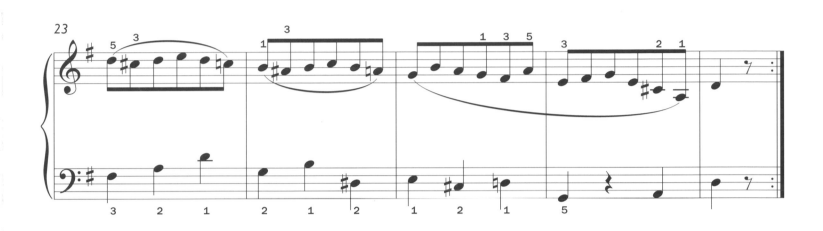

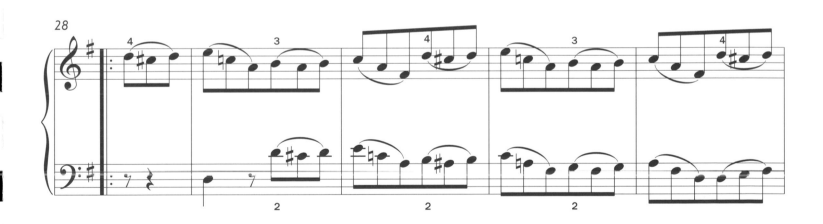

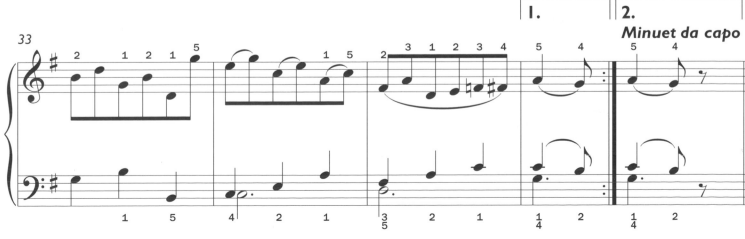

Nocturne in E Flat, Op.9, No.2

Music by Frédéric Chopin

Andante

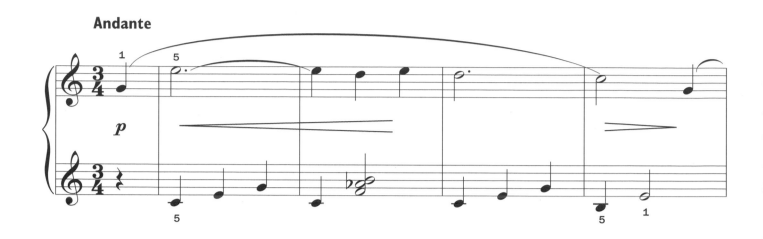

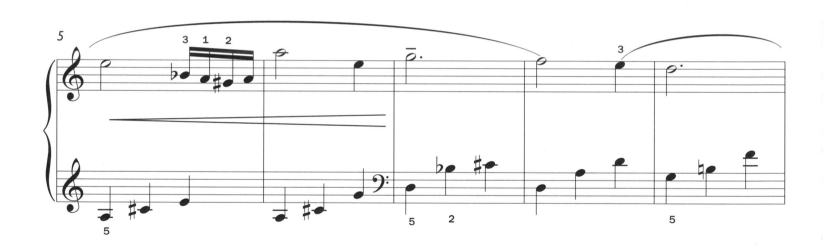

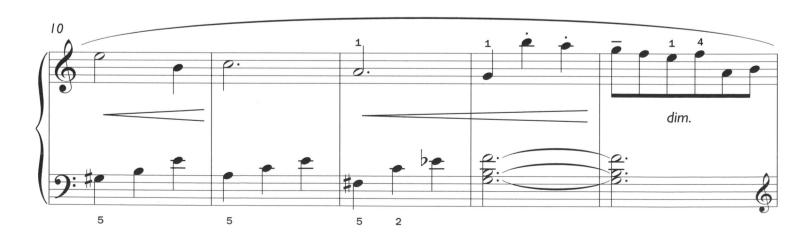

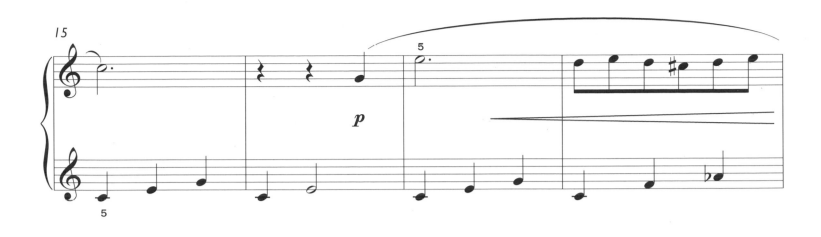

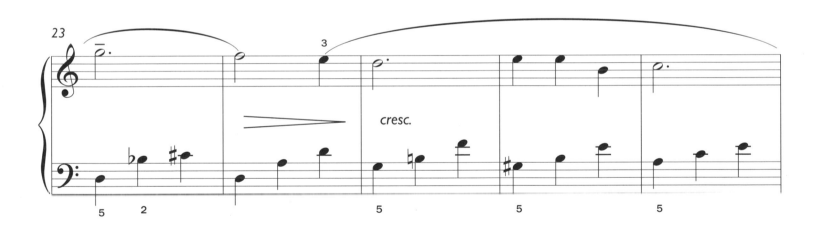

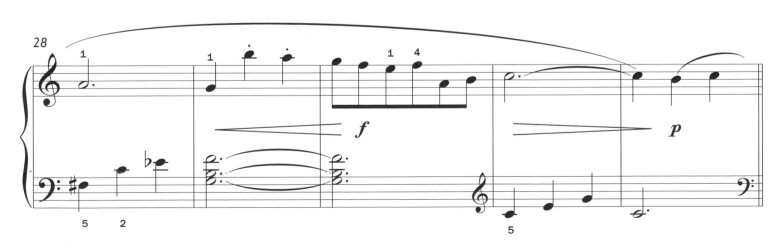

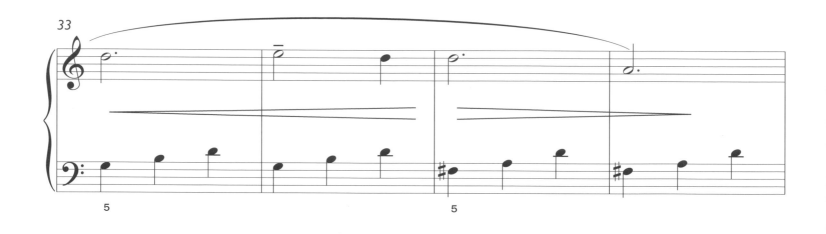

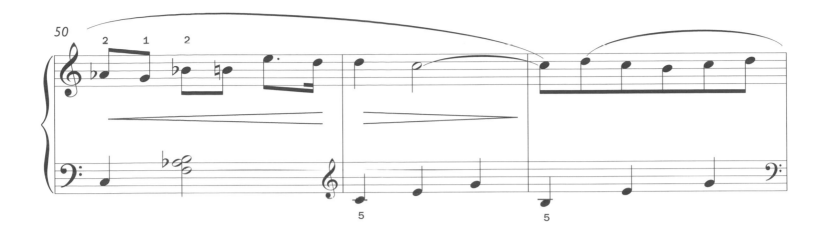

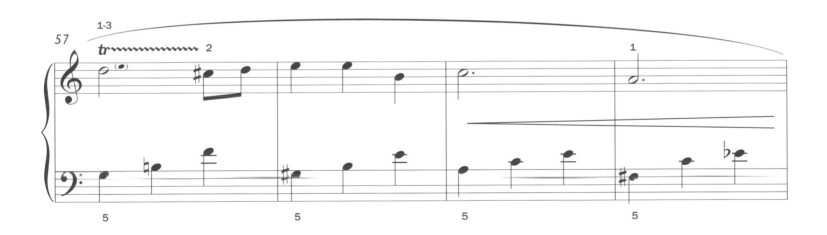

rit.

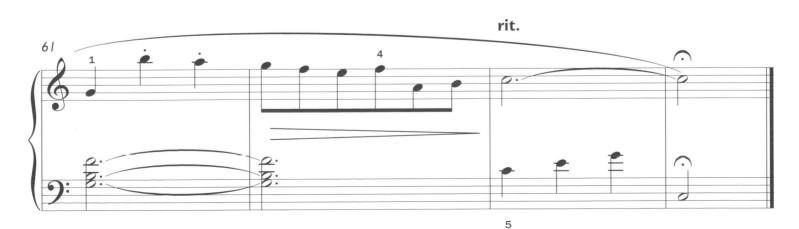

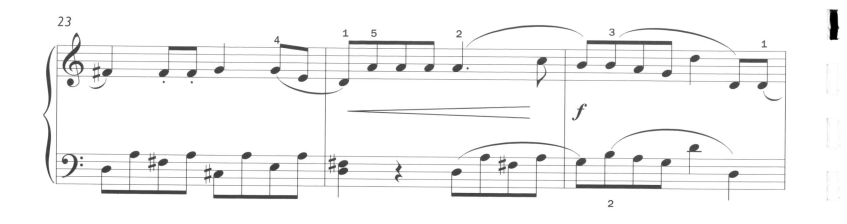

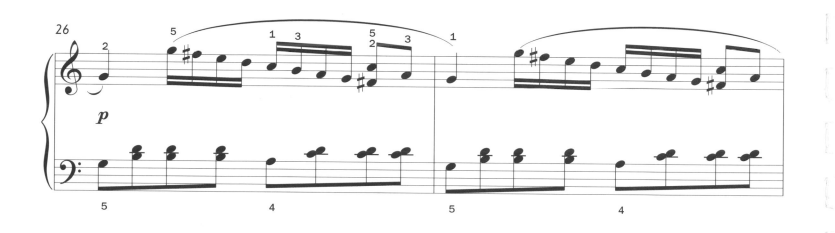

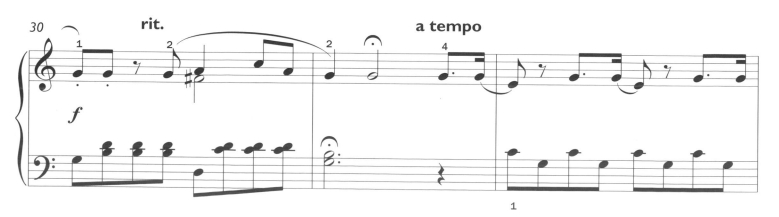

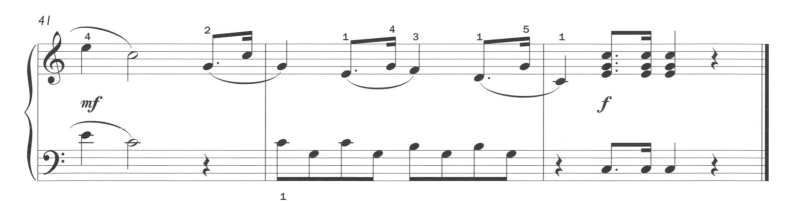

Panis Angelicus

Music by César Franck

Adagio

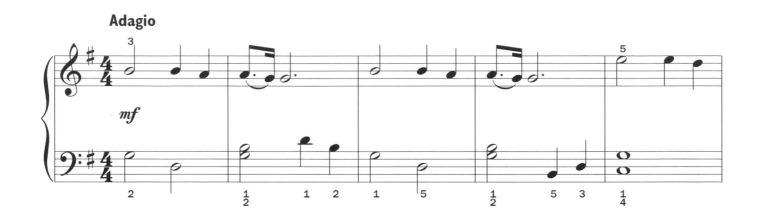

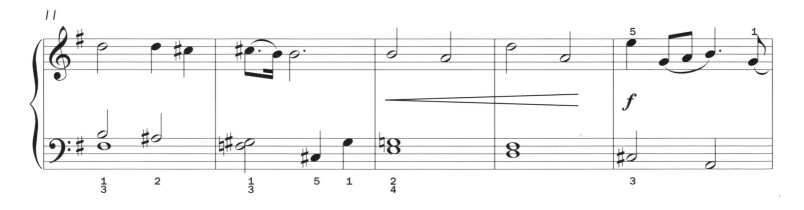

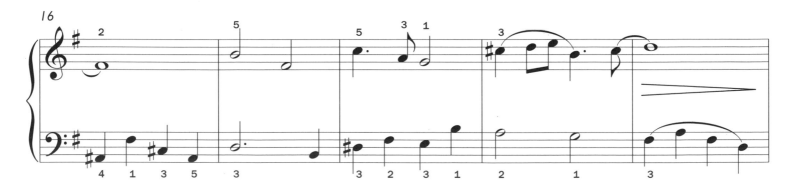

Liebestraume: Notturno No.3

Music by Franz Liszt

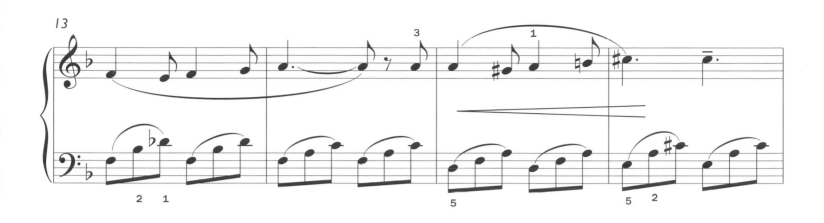

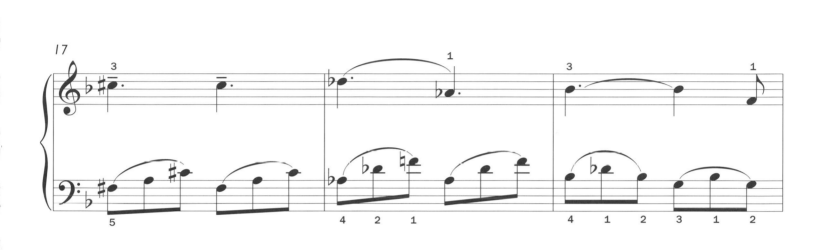

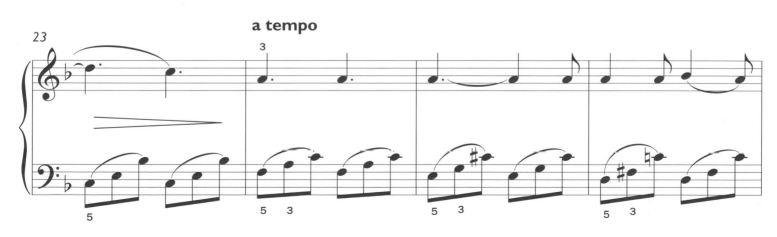

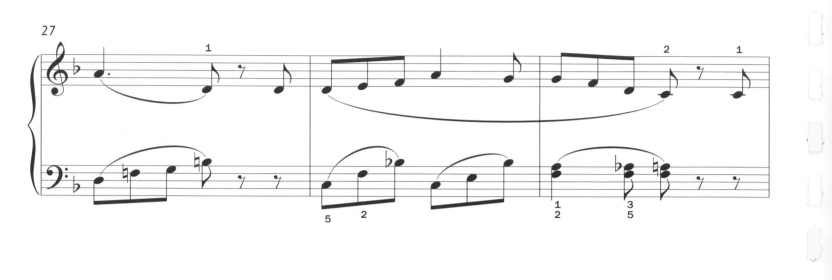

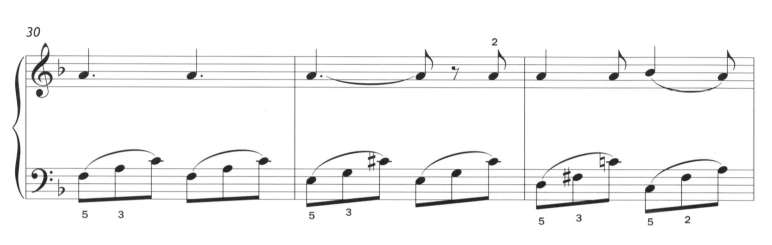

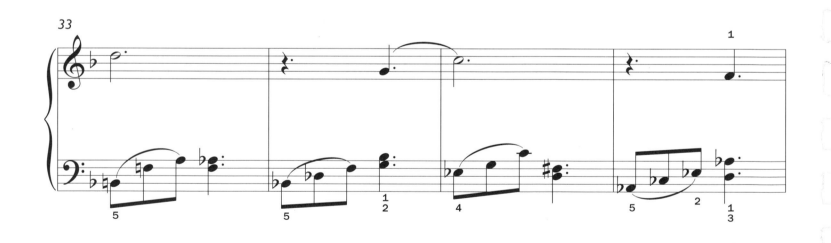

rit.

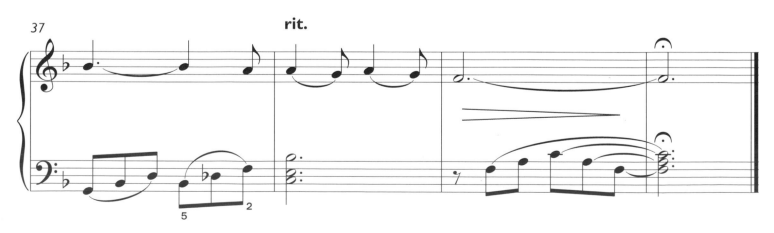

Promenade
(from 'Pictures At An Exhibition')

Music by Modest Mussorgsky

Allegro giusto, nel modo Russico, senza allegreza, ma poco sostenuto

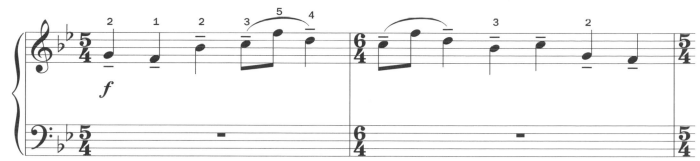

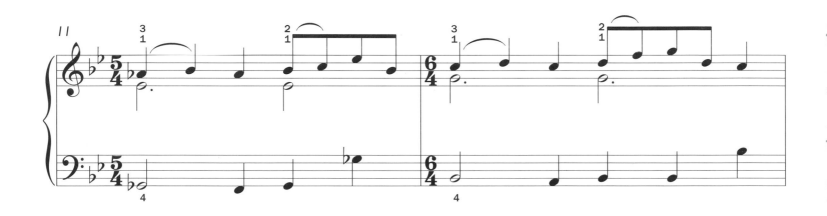

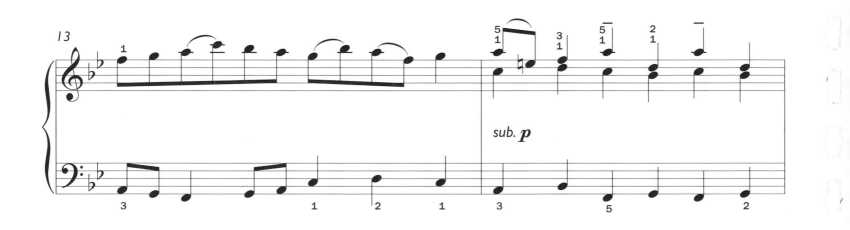

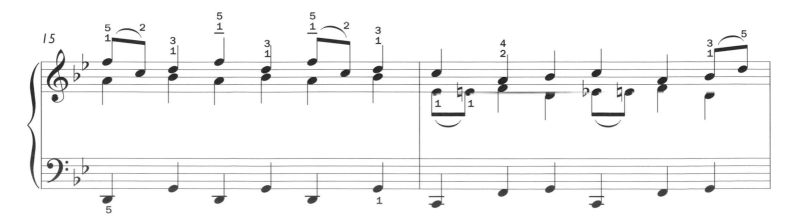

Prelude No.1 in C

Music by Johann Sebastian Bach

Moderato e legato

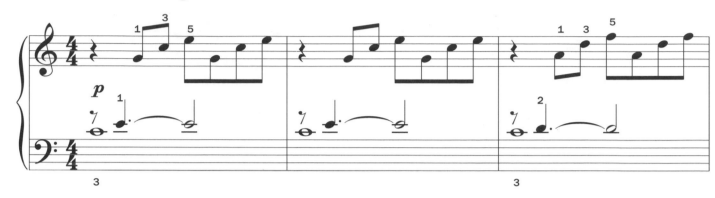

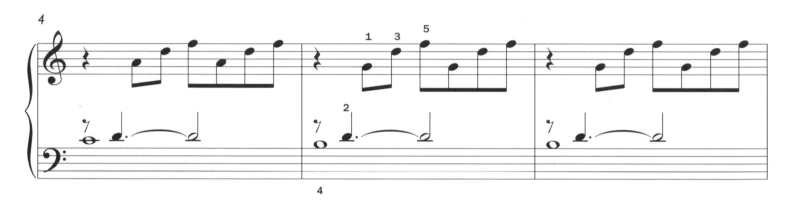

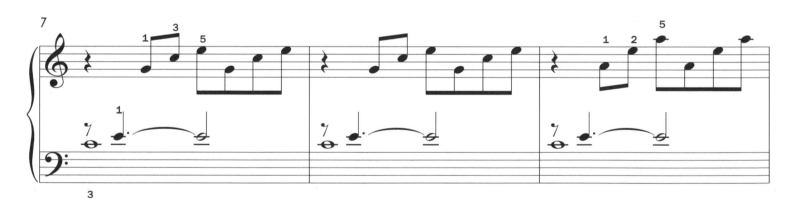

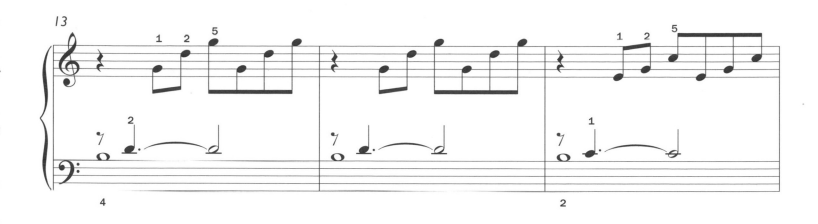

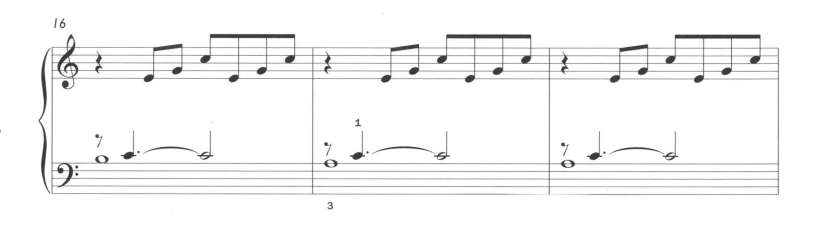

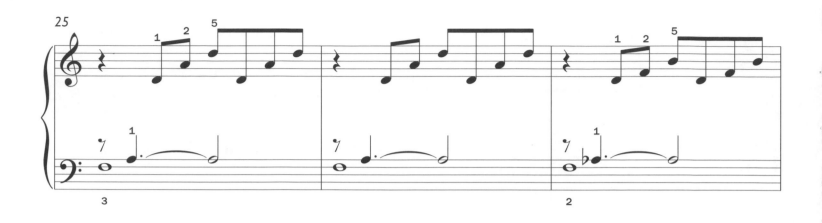

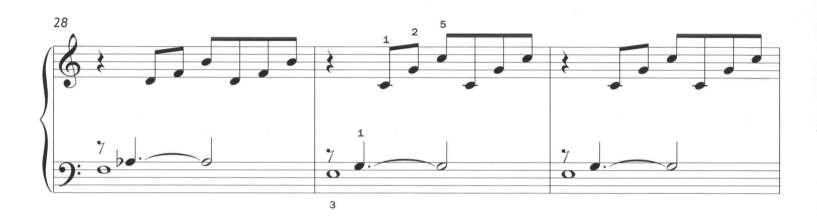

Romeo & Juliet

Music by Pyotr Ilyich Tchaikovsky

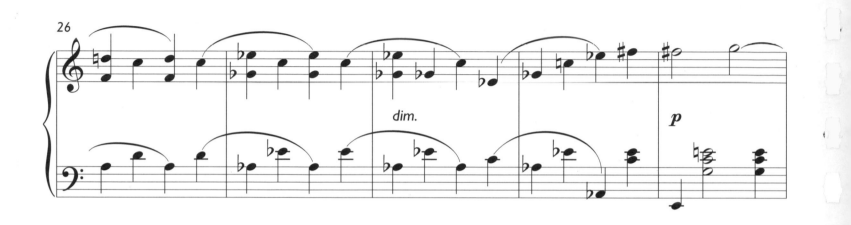

cresc.

Spring Song

Music by Felix Mendelssohn Bartholdy

Allegretto grazioso ♩ = c.88

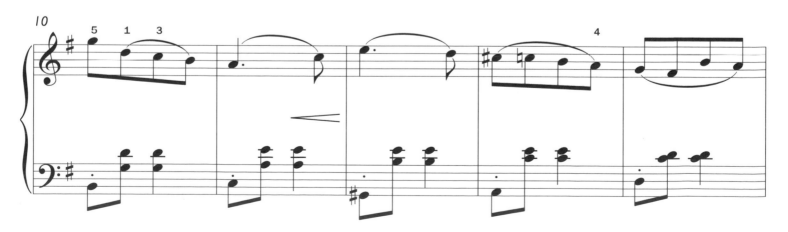

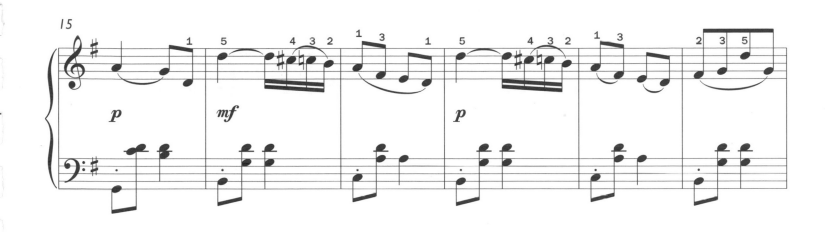

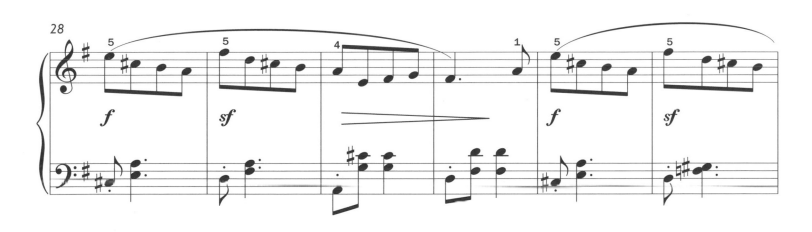

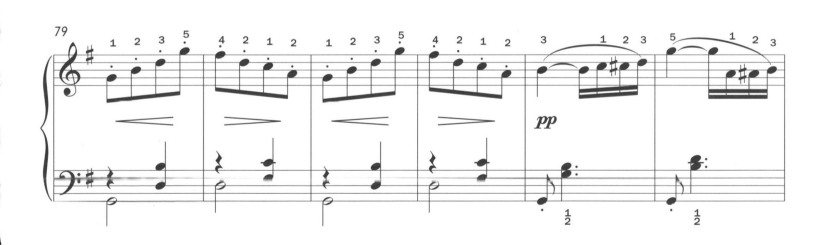

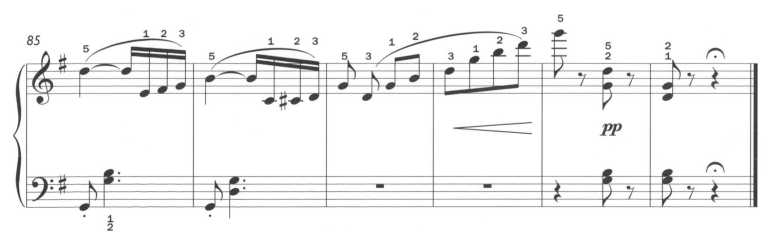

Theme
(from 'Swan Lake')

Music by Pyotr Ilyich Tchaikovsky

Träumerei

Music by Robert Schumann

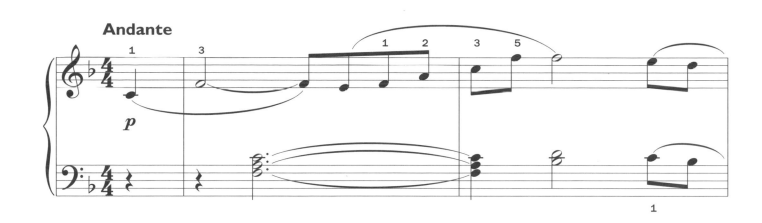

Toreador's Song
(from 'Carmen')

Music by Georges Bizet

Trout Quintet

Music by Franz Schubert

Andantino

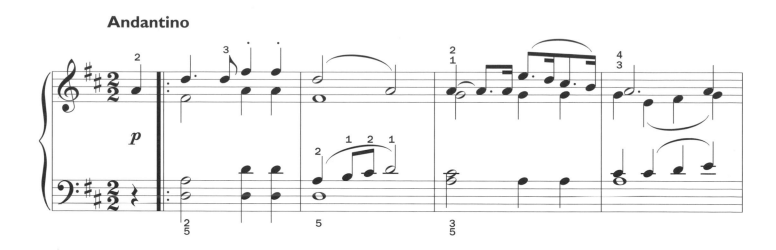

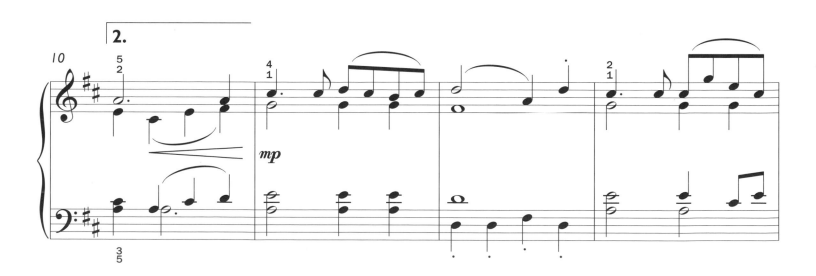

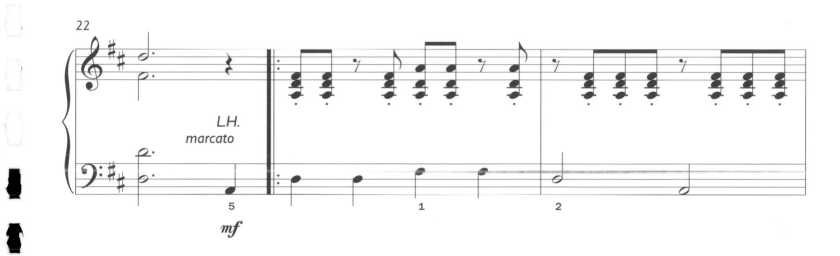

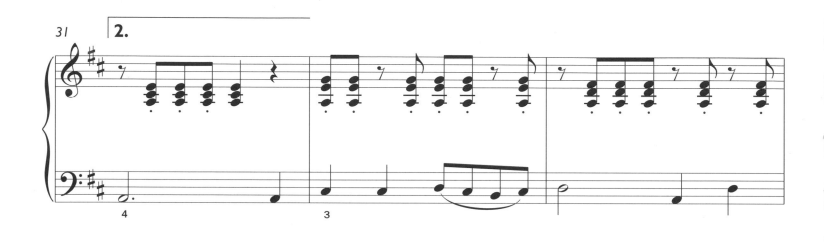

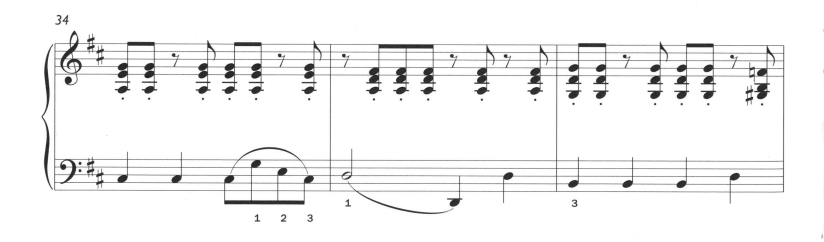

Symphony No.94 'Surprise'
(2nd movement)

Music by Franz Joseph Haydn

Andante

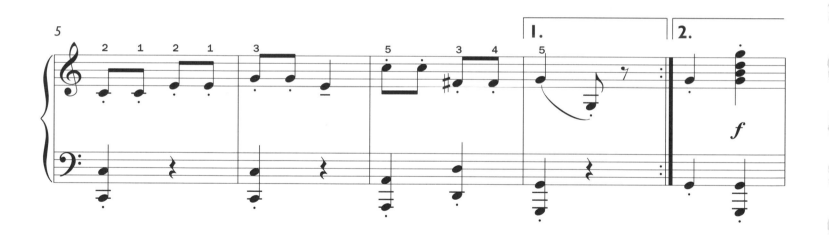

Theme
(from 'The Unfinished Symphony')

Music by Franz Schubert

Moderato

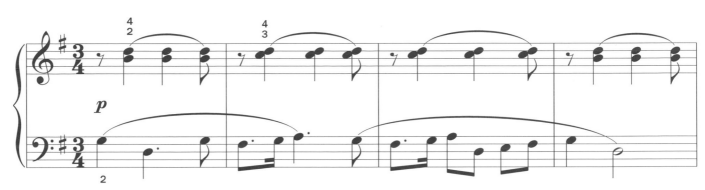

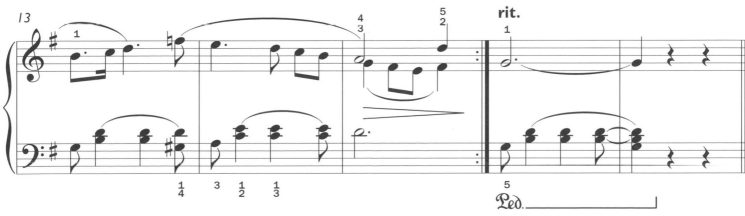

When I Am Laid In Earth
(from 'Dido And Aeneas')

Music by Henry Purcell

Larghetto

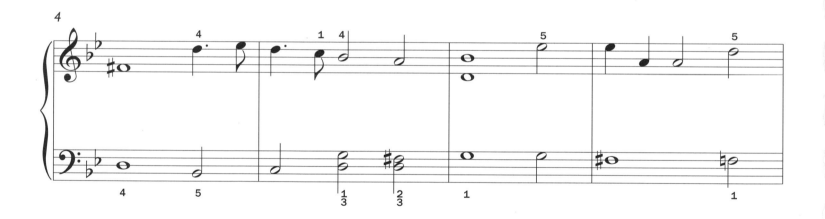

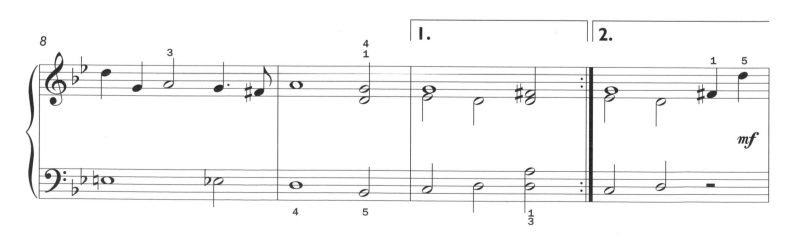

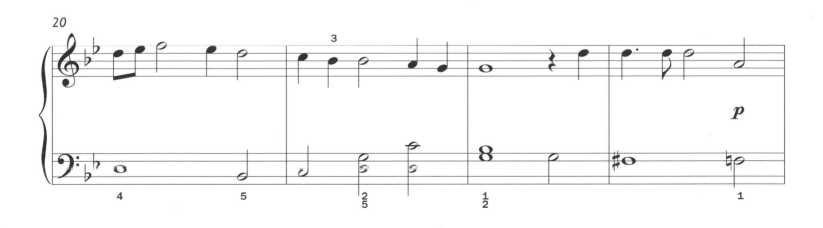

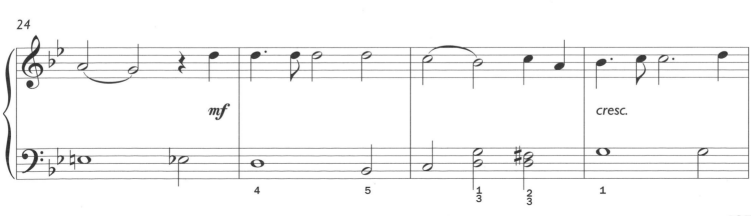

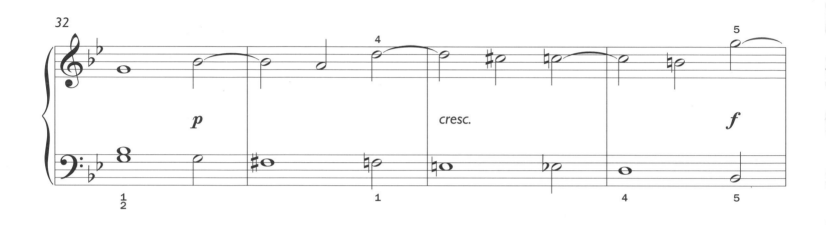

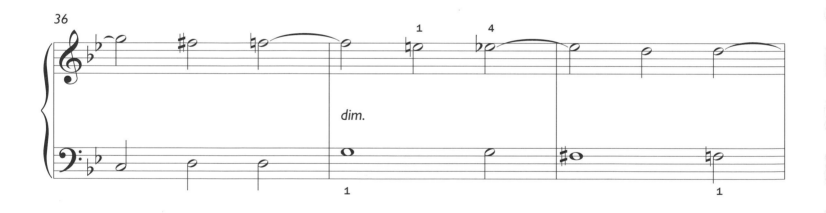

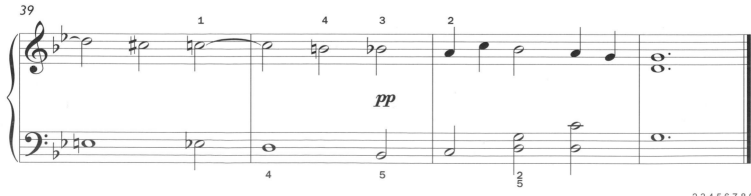

2 3 4 5 6 7 8 9
1/09(168328)